LIVING ABROAD - BINGO OR DISASTER

Bloomington, IN   authorHOUSE™   Milton Keynes, UK

AuthorHouse™
1663 Liberty Drive, Suite 200
Bloomington, IN 47403
www.authorhouse.com
Phone: 1-800-839-8640

AuthorHouse™ UK Ltd.
500 Avebury Boulevard
Central Milton Keynes, MK9 2BE
www.authorhouse.co.uk
Phone: 08001974150

First published by AuthorHouse 3/16/2006

ISBN: 1-4259-1192-7 (e)
ISBN: 1-4259-1190-0 (sc)

Printed in the United States of America
Bloomington, Indiana

This book is printed on acid-free paper.

Profile of the Ideal Expatriate and the Sharing of Our Experience Abroad
Part I

Profile

1. The main attributes of the ideal expatriate candidate are:
- has an entrepreneurial attitude,
- does not request, upon departure from his home country, job guarantees after the return from foreign assignments,
- loves change and is highly flexible,
- has a positive can-do attitude with a passion for enjoying the moment rather than worrying about the future or living in past memories,
- easily settles down in foreign environments and new jobs,
- has high social competencies,
- loves commuting between cultures and has a high degree of respect for different cultures,
- is married preferably to a partner of the same culture and preferably has no children,
- is proud of his/her roots in the country of origin,
- invests in property in the country of origin or in the country of planned retirement.

In short, he/she is somebody who loves to ride the wave rather than sailing behind it.

Incentives for expatriates to leave their countries of origin are very different. Most of my successful expatriate colleagues were motivated by the substantially increased remuneration, a curiosity to discover and test new limits, as well as to fast-track their managerial and professional expertise.

A recipe for an immediate crash landing abroad is fleeing from an issue in the country of origin (such as disappointments with relationships, financial difficulties, criminal charges, etc.).

We ventured abroad at the age of thirty-four because Switzerland was short of challenges and we wanted to discover new limits. From our employer's point of view, we were a reasonably good deal, because there were only the two of us without children. More often than expected, children make expatriates' careers less flexible due to the children's education. It can also become a cost issue for the employer, because education abroad is expensive, larger accommodations are required, home leaves become more expensive, and costs for relocation or repatriation are substantially higher.

2. Before Going Abroad

- Get cross-cultural training with the aim to tune the expatriate's as well as the partner's commitment to much-needed adaptability and flexibility.
- Tailor the remuneration package to the employee's specific situation.
- Pay particular attention to the requirements of the partner and the family.

2.1. CROSS-CULTURAL PREPARATION

A new assignment in a foreign environment can produce a great shock (called culture shock) to expatriates, the partner, and family. Expatriates also have to be made aware of each country's different business cultures and the different ways of achieving goals. The understanding of the cultural sensitivity of the host country is clearly an advantage before you go abroad. Although the business language might be English, it is a must to learn the basics of the local language of the host country prior to departure. Once arrived in the host country, you will find little time to learn the local language but ample opportunities to practice and enhance what you learned before your departure.

2.2.   TAILORED REMUNERATION PACKAGE

Each package needs careful consideration, taking into consideration home and host countries' specific issues—e.g., should the salary's currency deviate from the expatriate's reference currency in the home country, the protection from exchange-rate fluctuations, tax implications, etc. Likewise, allowances, such as for housing, club memberships, drivers, home leaves, and health-care protections, need to be tailored to the expatriate's specific situation. Not to be forgotten are the tax-related issues, which more often than not create serious friction between expatriates and employers if they are not carefully attended to by a tax attorney in the host country prior to the signing of a contract.

2.3.   PARTNER AND THE FAMILY

Family concerns and/or the partner's dissatisfaction are the main reasons for a premature termination of an expatriate's assignment. In many cases, the partner has to give up a career, adding to the problem of a family's decreased income. The schooling of children should be linked to the expatriate's strategy to either stay abroad or return to the home country.

3. Returning To Your Country Of Origin

My best piece of advice to all parties concerned is: Do not expect any guarantee, neither from the employer nor from the expatriate. The expatriate and employer should in principle agree to continue their relationship upon completion of the assignment, but that is it. Most expatriates tremendously change their perspective when abroad, which will be neither compatible to the home country nor to their own personal view at the time of departure.

Living abroad changes you in ways that will cause you to never again relate to your own culture in the same sense. When you go back, you will find that your friends have not changed as much as you have changed. In your expatriate world, so much happened, and you develop an appreciation for cultural differences foreign to your old friends and family.

Hence, my advice for expatriates and their employers is to manage the return to the expatriate's own roots in a pragmatic manner and with an awareness of the cultural differences and much-changed view of the expatriate.

I observed that a number of multinational companies do not realize their investments in expatriates. Expatriates greatly enhance their communication skills, cultural intelligence, as well as managerial skills while abroad, and such skills should be exploited for the successful business development within the group. It is a fact that most expatriates change employers upon the completion of their assignments abroad— what a waste of an investment from the employer's point of view.

Upon the return of the expatriate to the country of origin, I urge both parties concerned to be patient with each other. The reverse culture shock will hit most returning expatriates, which may well be more traumatic than the culture shock experienced in host countries.

The majority of expatriates returning to their home countries find it difficult to integrate again into the company and even their home country. Some of the expatriates also just lose the appetite to successfully deal with organizational politics. A successful integration can be achieved with a successful relocation policy under one roof of the multinational company taking care of the ever-changing needs of an international business community.

Let us now walk through my expatriate career. It is a roller coaster career starting in Indonesia, moving to Malaysia, Greece, India, the

Philippines, returning to India, moving to Switzerland (country of origin), and returning to Indonesia.

The Sharing of Our Experience Abroad

―――――◆◆◆―――――

Indonesia, 1984 to 1989

1. Political and economic environment
Mr. Suharto, the president of Indonesia, ruled the country with an iron fist in his military dictatorship. Yet the economy was rapidly developing with the support of foreign investments, in particular from Japan and USA.

2. Our group
Our group was an icon in the global insurance industry with a AAA rating and was committed to a decentralized management structure.

TOTALLY UNPREPARED—A JUMP INTO VERY COLD WATER

Although we extensively traveled around the world, we were simply not prepared to successfully place ourselves in this very different cultural environment. The daily English news lasted just twenty minutes and could be best described as the government's views rather than news. The expatriate communities were very close to each other, because each of them needed each other's support. Hence, the social life among expatriates played a vital part, and home entertainment formed an integral part of a successful expatriate assignment in Indonesia.

A START WITH AN AVOIDABLE MISTAKE

We arrived in Jakarta on a Friday 13th, and I went straight from Halim Airport to the funeral of my executive colleague's mother. From the Western cultural point of view, to attend such a funeral seems a matter of sympathy, but it was certainly wrong from my JV partner's cultural point of view.

As if Friday 13th would not have been bad luck enough, I greeted my Chinese colleague at the coffin of his mother, his face all in tears. What a mistake. I should have instead enjoyed a shower at the Borobudur Hotel and thereafter sent to his mother's home the nicest wreath covered with golden ornaments accompanied with our group's deepest sympathy.

Anybody aware of the special status of a mother within a Chinese family would have done so. In the absence of cultural preparation by our company, I acted according to my inherent cultural values, which were not quite compatible with the Chinese cultural value system.

This very wrong behavior shaped the relationship for the years ahead with my executive colleague, and he often reminded me of this event. He deeply believed that I brought bad luck and bad fortune to the company as well as to his family.

This experience made me instantly aware of important differences in cultural value systems, which are the key for successful management within a multicultural environment.

BEAUTIFUL IN ONE CULTURE MAY WELL BE UGLY IN ANOTHER CULTURE

Back in 1984, the lack of professional expertise made the international community in Indonesia rather sizeable. It was a boiling pot of interesting people with very different cultural backgrounds and many of them from cross-cultural marriages.

Communication within such a sensitive cultural environment becomes a delicate affair. It could well be that the person you are talking with would have a perfect Western face. But he or she could have grown up within a Chinese, Indian, or Malay environment or married into a cross-cultural partnership or just separated from such a partner.

Therefore, religious, political, and cultural issues are a no-no in any discussion, and such comments should only be shared within the circle of known friends.

What one culture considers as correct or beautiful may well be the opposite of the other culture's point of view. This reminds me of one of our Indonesian friends whom we much appreciated. She was a well-educated, graceful Indonesian lady who considered a German as very attractive because of his rather oversized pale body. From our cultural point of view, he fell far short of a handsome appearance, but she married him because of his white skin and his oversized body well three times her size.

It also reminds me of a friend of mine whose father was German, but he grew up in Hong Kong within a Chinese environment. Today he thinks and acts like the Chinese but looks like a European. Feng shui is much closer to him than European values, and it takes a while to get adjusted to such complexity.

DO NOT ATTEMPT TO CHANGE LOCAL DOS AND DON'TS BUT MANAGE THEM

Corruption in any form was omnipresent in Indonesia, and we quickly accepted it as a way of life. Every morning before I left home in Pondok Indah on my journey to the office at Hayam Wuruk, my shirt's pocket was loaded with some rupiah notes for distribution within the day to various parties. Sometimes I even reached the office without one single note left in my pocket, which made me feel like a soldier behind an unloaded gun.

I remember a policeman overtaking us on his bike, requesting in the most polite manner that we stop by the roadside. He reminded us that my driver had passed the traffic light while red. Hence, I skillfully shook hands with the police officer with some rupiah in my palm, but his body language revealed disappointment. He again waved us back to the traffic jam, and only a few kilometers down the road, the very same police officer again approached us with the same claim.

I instantly understood—the same procedure as last time. Certainly I could have objected to his second or even first claim with the consequence that my driver would have had to submit his driver's license on the spot with the request to collect it again next week. Guess what I did. I again shook hands with the policeman but this time with the appropriate amount of money.

TIME. WHAT THE HELL IS THAT IN INDONESIA?

Caucasians usually strive to be punctual regardless of their social ranking, whereas in many Asian cultures, it is a must that the most important person or the guest of honor be the last to join the party. This unwritten rule reminds me of a conductor who will join his orchestra as soon as the audience has been seated. But unlike with the orchestra, the delay in Asia might be hours. The longest I stood around until the guest of honor arrived was above four hours. Such a delay should not be interpreted as impolite but indicates the perceived social status. My advice is: Be never punctual; otherwise, you might have to assist the waiters with the buffet.

THE RIGHT NETWORK CAN BE MAGIC

Back in 1985, mobile telephones did not exist, and it was common in posh areas, like Pondok Indah, that your landline was disconnected, most likely prior to the festive Muslim season of Ramadan. The secret to a successful reconnection was to leverage your links to government officials with a reasonable or more-often unreasonable fee.

In our case, it was even worse, because at our first residence we never received a landline telephone. And this was simply because of our landlord's personal dispute with our neighbor who leveraged his connection to the public telephone authority to our disadvantage.

Our Chinese landlord insulted the neighbor, who was of Malay origin. The Malay culture, based on harmony and respect, does not tolerate unsettled personal disputes, and it will overrule business sense. No matter how hard we tried, we simply did not get the landline, and I decided to get a mobile telephone station from Singapore. It was not a comparable size of today's mobile telephones. It consisted of two bulky handsets, two ten-meter aerials, a powerful amplifier, and sixty meters of cable. The point is that telecommunication equipment was banned from imports to Indonesia, and I could ill hide such bulky equipment at the point of entry in Indonesia.

My local network was granting me red-carpet treatment upon my arrival at the airport. I was welcomed right at the exit of the aircraft and patiently accompanied at the conveyor belt for the collection of my suitcases, and we walked through immigration with a smile "by all parties involved." Certainly such special treatment had its price tag, but without connection to this network, our posting without a telephone would have been very difficult, mainly due to security concerns.

The same network at customs worked much to our benefit some months later and saved my direct superior from a major embarrassment upon his arrival in Indonesia.
Margrit earlier smuggled to Indonesia a lovebird, or Agapornis (a small parrot), well aware of the fact that parrots or even parts of parrots are banned from imports to Indonesia due to the parrot disease. As long as a bird is in a dark compartment, it will not whistle, and Margrit gave her parrot a lift in her handbag right through immigration.

But our parrot, Stritzi, passed away after one year, and my direct superior wanted to surprise Margrit with a replacement.

Unfortunately, upon his arrival, the parrots also greeted the customs officers, and their melody invited the customs officers to negotiate the deal of their lives with a first-class passenger violating the immigration law of Indonesia. I took note of the negotiations, and the customs officer who accompanied me some months ago through immigration with my communication equipment was also on duty. I approached him, and we were able to amicably solve the matter within a couple of minutes.

Indonesia taught me how important it is to foster relationships, and being part of the right local networks can make a difference to your stay in a foreign country.

THE CULTURE SHOCK WILL KNOCK YOU DOWN, BUT DO NOT REMAIN TOO LONG ON THE CANVAS

At the very beginning, we felt homesick watching the planes flying over our house and wishing to be in them. But being homesick is natural at your first assignment abroad and part of the culture shock expatriates are experiencing.

The culture shock can be best described as a paralyzing period of time during which you decline the host country's culture. You perceive the differences to your inherent culture just as too great to manage. Let me share with you some experiences of this phenomenon.

One of my passions in Europe was to read many newspapers, but the censorship in Indonesia did not make reading much of a pleasure. Any non state-conform political, religious, or social reference to Indonesia was overprinted with a black color. This color stuck also on the opposite page, and more often than not, I ended up with a patchwork of newspaper pages. Also, Margrit's female magazines from Europe were censored, and any topless advertisement was skillfully overprinted with this black color. It must have been quite an experience to those "censors," who most probably got their relief thereafter at some nightclub. For months I got excited each day instead of just accepting that this was now the way it was in my host country.

I remember being on the golf course in Pondak Indah together with Margrit and our caddies. We were all alone, and out of the blue, an army officer of Malay origin approached us with his firm request to instantly stop our game, because Mr. Suharto, the president of Indonesia, was approaching our flight from the rear. For security reasons, the officer explained, he had to make sure that between the president and any flight there was a vacant distance of two holes. We had no choice but to let Mr. Suharto's flight pass with eight caddies, four of them carrying guns in their bags instead of clubs. His flight completely ignored us, passing by without extending the common courtesy on any golf course of saying "terima kashi" (thank you) for passing a flight.

The point I wish to make here is that any extreme cultural behavior should not be answered with adverse actions leading to unexpected reactions. Just stay calm and do not react—no matter how much it will hurt your ego.

An extreme behavior in the Chinese culture shocked me in my initial years abroad with the murder of a distant friend of mine who broke the trust of his business partner. Without further discussing the issue, he was murdered, and his family was even informed of the reason for his early departure.

We were very fortunate to immediately find friends of whom a number were married to Indonesians either of Malay or Chinese origin. The Malay culture, which is based on harmony and respect, has little in common with the Chinese culture within its world of money, superstition, trust, and food. With this understanding and our progress with the local language, we gradually were able to manage the culture shock and respect and understand the differences to our inherent culture.

DOMESTIC STAFF DOES NOT JUST ASSIST YOU BUT IS ALSO A HEALTH RISK TO YOUR FAMILY

Home entertainment was very important and vital for a successful business development. Therefore, a number between five and ten servants often formed part of an expatriate's family. There were just the two of us without children, and therefore, we could manage our social life with a smaller crew of five: a cook, a houseboy, a gardener, and two drivers. We only employed male servants because the moment a female helper entered the team, the boys had some other points on their agenda. On the other hand, male servants hardly ever became pregnant.

Yet we had five of them, and it is worth the while to also share our experiences on this subject.

Sudrisno, our first cook, learned his profession on a cruise ship and brought, therefore, a wealth of international experience with him. We became the favorite spot for home entertainment mainly because of his cooking skills and charming way of attending to guests. He went twice a week to the fish market, and we ate fresh seafood of the best quality until such a point in time that Margrit became allergic to seafood. After a dinner, Margrit complained about itching, and the following shower made her eyelids swollen. She looked like a frog. Her whole body gained in size, and we rushed to the hospital.

There were just a few medical doctors around. Traffic jams disallow fast medical attention, and once at the hospital, you will find more often than not outdated medical equipment and indecisive medical attention.

Sudrisno was a great cook, but his cultural background somehow disallowed him to fully respect a woman junior to him as his direct superior. After three years of service, we had to often correct him, and in his effort to restore the working relationship with Margrit, he decided to apply an ancient recipe. We noticed that Margrit had a number of infections, which puzzled us, until we discovered the source for such infections. The reason was our cook served Margrit's coffee with his saliva in her cup. According to his belief, he wanted to restore his relationship with Margrit by mixing his saliva with Margrit's while she was enjoying her espresso. Quite innovative because he could ill afford to kiss "the boss" and instead spit into her coffee.

The health risk from people working in your household cannot be ignored, and we shared a number of similar stories with our expatriate friends. It is important to make them wash their hands whenever they enter the kitchen (because some cultures use their hands instead of tissues in the bathroom), provide them with effective medicine, and send them to monthly medical checkups at the hospital of your choice together with their immediate family members.

DON'T FORGET TO ALSO ENJOY THE MOMENT WITHIN A DIFFERENT CULTURAL ENVIRONMENT

On a lighter note, we often could laugh about our servants. They asked us to get money for a ladder in order to attend to some repair work on the roof. After a few days, the ladder was completed, and we were asked to admire the pretty long ladder of about five meters. With pride, they invited us to the inauguration, but they could not even lift it up because the hardwood they used made the ladder too heavy.

The backyard of our house was rather exposed to unexpected visitors who occasionally climbed the wall rather out of curiosity than the intention to burglarize our house. We were kind of disturbed by such acts, and I purchased, during one of our home leaves in Switzerland, an electrical fence charger, which is used for keeping the cows in their intended eating area. I erected two wires on top of the wall, and the sound of the first climber who touched the fence is still fresh in my memory. Quickly the rumor spread that one single touch would kill the strongest person, and as of that date, we were liberated from any unexpected visitors in the backyard.

Claudio used a more-bloody method. He positioned his Doberman dog in the backyard after sunset, and indeed one night the dog killed a man who tried to get access to the backyard. I still consider my method as the more effective one and certainly the cleaner version.

An English expatriate friend asked his servants to clean the carpets during his home leave and was surprised at a thorough job upon his arrival. The result was disastrous because they washed all of them in the washing machine. Not quite an advisable method for silk carpets.

An Irish colleague asked his houseboy to paint the whole room white during his home leave. Upon his arrival, the houseboy proudly presented the room all in white, including all the wooden furniture.

But one of the most enjoyable experiences we shared during a dinner. A wall that had an opening—a hatch—separated the kitchen from the dining area. Through such an opening, the hot dishes could find their speedy way to the table. Hence, the host reminded his cook to pass the food through the hatch in order to benefit from hot plates. He immediately followed his boss's advice, returned to the kitchen, and crawled together with the food through the hatch.

STRICTLY NO COMMENT ON POLITICAL OR SOCIAL ISSUES OF YOUR HOST COUNTRY

ISCI's rugby section was well known for its great parties with a lot of beer and beautiful Indonesian women. During one of its annual gatherings at Mandarin Hotel, the president of the rugby section proposed a toast to Madam 10%, which was the nickname of President Suharto's wife. She was indeed a unique personality with a humble appearance and expensive fabrics neither matching bag nor shoes. In the same humble way, she also requested from many business deals a 10 percent contribution directed to her bank account. This was common knowledge among the business community, but nobody would dare to publicly address this subject except an American who proposed his famous toast. I guess he just drank a couple of whiskies too many, and within minutes of his famous toast, the army surrounded the Mandarin Hotel. He was declared persona non grata and had to leave the country within a couple of days.

Foreigners have to be extremely careful in their public behavior, which is carefully watched or supervised by the local community. And nationalism more often than not overrules friendships to foreign nationals.

JAPANESE EXCLUSIVELY BUY FROM JAPANESE

Pondok Indah Golf Club was increasingly crowed by Koreans and Japanese, and we, the Caucasians and Indonesians, were all of a sudden in the minority. During this period of time, I got to learn the Japanese and Korean culture and above all their creative skills of moving the positions of their balls in bunkers as well as on fairways. Some Japanese spent more time on the golf course than in the office and yet earned a decent income. After a round of golf, I mentioned to a Japanese man that we were not able to penetrate the Japanese market segment despite most favorable terms. He smiled behind his hand covering his red face (red because of beer, not the sun), and he replied that I would never succeed. He continued. "If you want to be successful with Japanese companies, you have to know where to get the most beautiful Indonesian girls for business partners, to drink long hours with them, as well as to share many rounds of golf. Certainly," he said, "you could do all of that, but the most important key success factor you cannot present to Japanese companies, which is a Japanese face."

DO NOT MISS THE PLANE IN CASE OF EMERGENCY

The years 1985/86 were years of political unrest, which was suppressed by Suharto's iron fist. Still fresh to my memory are many arson cases at shopping centers such as Sharina Jaya at Thamrin Road and at Block M, followed by the powerful explosion of the ammunition dump in Cilandak. This dump was rather close to Pondok Indah, and during the hours-long explosions, we did not know what actually happened. Were we at war, or was it directed against the wealthier community living in Pondok Indah?

We heard missiles flying in an uncoordinated manner over our house, and it was quite a relief to hear the impact of any missile—thankfully not on me. The most frightening part was to wait for the next missile starting its journey to an unknown destination.

In a rush, we collected our passports, money, flight tickets, and dog, and drove in our car toward Bogor. All the way, we heard the missiles exploding behind us. Under some high trees on the way to Bogor, we finally found shelter, stopped our car, and spent the night in our car. The next morning, we were afraid to return to our house, which we feared to be on fire or burglarized. To our surprise, our house was undamaged, though others were not that lucky.

During this difficult period of time, most of the foreign community was lost without a great chance for a timely escape to safer destinations like Singapore or Hong Kong. We always had an open ticket with a preferred booking arrangement with one of the airlines.

Lucky us, we never had to experience a mass evacuation, but we did experience one emergency leave with Margrit to Singapore. She was under the medical attention of an Indonesian medical doctor who simply reacted too late to Margrit's dehydration. I was the one calling the ambulance, and Margrit got the attention of professional nurses at the hospital. They provided me with the necessary equipment and life-saving nutrition over which I was asked to assume control that night. I even had to search for a new battery pack for the medical equipment, and I still wonder how we made it through that night. It would have been mission impossible without being able to communicate in the local language and to coordinate the following evacuation to Singapore.

THIRST IN TROPICAL CLIMATES SHOULD BE KILLED EXCLUSIVELY WITH WATER

Whenever I returned from work, Goldy (our Indonesian cross-breed dog) would first greet me, followed by Sudrisno's question: "Sir, what would you like to drink?" He served some drinks at the bar prior to dinner, and I had to stop this procedure, because we took note of a typical "expatriate disease," the liking of alcohol. The frequent social activities often make expatriates attached to the bottle. Unconsciously, expatriates slip into a mood of going to bed more often drunk than sober. The humid weather also makes some drinks a pleasant experience. Here a whisky soda, a gin, and there a bloody mary also helps to survive boring receptions. We were fortunate to recognize the danger and controlled our drinking habit, but for a number of our colleagues, it was too late.

LISTEN TO LOCAL ADVICE

Durian, an Asian fruit with a taste that you either love or hate, was our passion in Indonesia. An objective description, if such a thing exists on something you call a passion, would be that the taste of a durian is a mixture between a very mature cheese and some nuts and onions. The smell is strong, and you are not allowed to enter an aircraft or restaurant with a durian because of its strong smell.

What a delicacy, which one day nearly turned into a fatal accident. Indonesians told us that we should never eat a durian and at the same time drink alcohol. This combination increases the buildup of gas during the fermentation process in your stomach, and you end up with a severe headache, which can result in death. Aware of such horror stories, we ignored local advice, and I enjoyed with a friend some durians, and together with the coffee we also drank a cognac. I found myself in bed for the following week. I lost more than 15 percent of my body weight and experienced the strongest headache of my life. Lucky me, I survived.

MANAGING THE DEPARTURE AND PREPARING YOURSELF FOR THE NEXT POSTING

On February 1, 1989, we had to leave Indonesia for Malaysia. On the same day, the container left our house, and we also left together with Goldy (our dog) to the new Sukarno Hatta airport. Due to the short distance to Malaysia, our transport to Kuala Lumpur only lasted a week, and therefore, we stayed at our house until the packers moved the container to the airport.

In retrospect, this was a mistake, which did not find its repetition in the following assignments. You need an emotional break between two assignments. Firstly, you should pack your household; thereafter, return your residence to the landlord followed by a stay of two weeks at a hotel. Within this period of time, you should attend the farewell parties of your friends and business contacts and only thereafter take the plane to your new assignment.

Such a procedure helps to shape the mindset and mental acceptance for the new assignment in your next country.

Malaysia, 1989 to 1993

1. Political and economic environment
In 1989, Malaysia emerged from a deep recession to an unprecedented economic boom. President Mahatir's benign dictatorship focused on upgrading the Bumiputras' standard of living (Malaysians of Malay origin) by granting them economic privileges, which were not given to their fellow nationals of Chinese or Indian origin.

2. Our group
Our group experienced a steady growth, and we were able to retain our AAA rating. The management style slowly shifted to a top-down management structure.

PETS MAY CREATE EMOTIONAL STRESS (FOR YOU AND YOUR PET)

Upon arrival in Malaysia, we had to take our dog to the quarantine for one month. We stayed at Hyatt Saujana Hotel, close to the quarantine, allowing Margrit to visit daily our dog, because Goldy simply refused to accept food and drinks from the personnel at the quarantine. The stress for animals during a quarantine of any length is not to be underestimated, and our dog was not the exception. We saw a number of animals passing away due to various reasons (vaccinations, wrong food, no attention, etc.) and many tears in expatriates' eyes.

WHAT AN EXPERIENCE TO MEET PEOPLE WHO SKIP TECHNOLOGIES

During our years in Malaysia, international communication was rapidly changing. In Indonesia, we communicated through telex, whereas Malaysians had never heard of such "obsolete technology." They just knew faxes, intranets, and the Internet. It seems that Malaysians skipped technology, and a typewriter was foreign to them, but they knew the keyboard of their PCs.

Together with the Internet, the first cellular phones appeared and rapidly gained popularity. They were not only very bulky but also expensive with a market even providing fake versions. Today it is quite unbelievable, but people were standing in hotel lobbies talking into fake cell phones, pretending to also belong to the wireless community.

In sharp contrast to Malaysia's technological environment, the situation in our office was quite different. Taking note of the desperate situation in the office, I wanted to relax on my chair and fell right over because one roller was missing. I could never figure out the original color of the carpet, and a vacuum cleaner was foreign to our offices. With the installation of the intranet, we also underlined the new strategic direction with a move to a more appropriate office location at Selangor Dredging Building.

SAME CULTURES, SAME RELIGION, AND YET SO DIFFERENT

In sharp contrast to Indonesia, Malaysia is underpopulated, and we again enjoyed some space around us. We often asked ourselves, "Where are the people?" Unlike Indonesia, Malaysia was an emerging market requesting us to adjust our way of life as expatriates.

What struck us most in Malaysia was the tense cultural relationship between Chinese, Indians, and Bumiputras (Malays of the same origin as the Malays in Indonesia). Although we already experienced the same cultures in Indonesia, the sharp difference in Indonesia is that the Chinese community was the clear minority, whereas in Malaysia, the ratio between Chinese and Bumiputras is close to

1:1. The privileges granted to the Bumiputra community (unequal treatment of two cultures with the same nationality) further increased the wide gap between these two cultures' understanding.

Also differently, we perceived the influence of Islam in both countries. Although Indonesia has one of the largest Muslim populations, Islam was not declared as a state religion. But in Malaysia, Islam was declared as its state religion, and it was felt in particular during Iraq's invasion of Kuwait in 1991. Malaysia stood firmly behind Saddam Hussein, and the foreign community was the declared enemy of a great number of Muslims in the country.

All Muslims were forced to adhere during Ramadan, fasting during daytime, whereas in Indonesia, the rules were not strictly followed. This religious belief led to low productivity and low blood-sugar levels, quite dangerous to people whose jobs required a high degree of concentration (programmers, drivers, etc.).

Also in sharp contrast to Indonesia, we could get in Kuala Lumpur most of our favorite food like cheese, whereas wine was rather difficult to get due to the Islamic influence.

<u>EACH CULTURE IS MOTIVATED BY ITS DISTINCTIVE VALUES</u>

It was a unique challenge to manage within the same company people of the same nationality (Malaysians) but of different cultural backgrounds (Malays, Chinese, Indians, and Portuguese). I carefully studied their different cultural value systems and motivated them according to their inherent cultures.

Any company outing was a logistic exercise and a challenge of its own. One culture disallows spouses to stay overnight without their partners, whereas the other culture welcomed the idea of being separated with a valuable reason. Or one culture cannot eat pork, whereas the other does not eat beef or any meat at all.

THOSE WERE THE GOLDEN YEARS OF ASIA

Our years in Malaysia were indeed the "golden years of Asia," and golf courses were mushrooming everywhere. We stayed at Damansara Heights, and within a thirty-minute drive, we had access to at least ten golf courses. Everybody earned a fair share of the economic boom, and I remember an annual 100 percent increase in our company's payroll with an unchanged number of employees. It was just very hard to keep well-qualified employees, which made the retention policy based on a cultural understanding the key for a successful business development.

During this period, the plans for the TV tower behind Shangri-La and Petronas' twin towers in Kuala Lumpur were designed, as was the new airport near Melaka.

IT IS IMPORTANT TO COMMUNICATE IN THE NATIVE LANGUAGE OF THE HOST COUNTRY

Due to my Bahasa Indonesian knowledge, a number of Malays welcomed discussions on issues that they were not able to discuss within their immediate families. They opened up to me because I spoke their native language. In particular, young women did not readily accept their families' influence, who wanted them to shape their future life according to Islamic values. Some of them had little choice but to leave their beloved families and migrate to any destination possible. Others surrendered to the pressure of the immediate and extended families and adjusted their lifestyles to Islamic values. Upon marriage, they exchanged their miniskirts for the traditional long dress and covered their hair with a veil. The great majority of this group of women immediately put on weight, and within a few months, their appearances had nothing in common with their pre-marriage appearances.

There were also exceptions, and I remember a fine lady who strictly followed the dress code but always stuck with fashionable shoes, perfect makeup, and artwork on her fingernails. It was her way of expressing her personality within the rules of her religion.

THE CULTURE SHOCK HIT US AGAIN

Upon the arrival of our container from Indonesia, I received a call from customs with the request to identify my container. I went there and could not believe what I saw. They completely unpacked the container, and most of the boxes were open. Certainly these were our goods, and the customs officer's particular attention found the large number of French wine bottles (Margaux 1982). I bought them from a Frenchman who was declared persona non grata in Indonesia. The customs officer reminded me that I would only be allowed to import wine for my personal consumption, but from his point of view, this great number of wine bottles rather represented Shangri-La's annual consumption. I insisted that I would not sell a single bottle and would enjoy all of them during my assignment in Malaysia. He finally gave in but also provided me with a powerful lesson of his religious background. He picked up at random six bottles from my "wine depot" and asked me to join him. We went to a large metal container with a rather strong smell of whisky, gin, and you name it. He demonstratively broke each of my six bottles on the edge of the container and threw them into the container. I looked at him in disbelief but stayed calm, although my blood was boiling with a heart rate close to 190. It was such a humiliating experience beyond description, and it took me some time to overcome the culture shock.

UNDERSTANDING THE FINE CULTURAL DIFFERENCES MAKES LIFE MUCH EASIER

Our house at Damansara Heights was between two Malaysian families but of different cultural origins. On the left-hand side lived a Chinese family and on the right-hand side a Malay family. They gave us a daily demonstration of their cultural differences and their cultural value systems.

The property of the Chinese family was all in concrete because it is less costly to maintain such a surface and can also be used as parking spaces for the many cars. It was amusing to watch how often they cleaned their cars. We never figured out the exact number of people living in house. Our count was between eight and nineteen, and the around-the-clock eating attracted rats that killed their thirst in our swimming pool. They focused on their family life, and other parties were not of much interest to them.

The Malay neighbors invested most of their time in the beautification of the house and the garden. One day, I met him flat on his back on the freshly cut lawn, and we shared an interesting conversation. He did not even get up from the lawn and explained that he always enjoyed the smell of freshly cut grass. Everything had to be in harmony, and they always wanted to assist us in whatever manner.

USE THE "CORPORATE TOURISM" TO YOUR ADVANTAGE FOR NETWORKING WITHIN YOUR GROUP

The management style in our group rapidly changed to a centralized management structure with a sudden increase of visitors from the corporate center (in particular during Europe's cold winter months). We were also the preferred spot for conferences, which allowed us to have some fun with the group's key executives unfamiliar with Asia and the opportunities for networking.I remember having dinner at Hyatt Saujana with one of the corporate center's executives, who admired the green color present everywhere.

He said, "Hermann, look at this tree, how green it is, just beautiful." "I do not quite know what tree you mean, but that one just in front of us is a banana tree," I replied. I wonder what they learn at Harvard, which was where he earned his PhDs (not just one).

We also shared a good time with key executives on a number of excursions, which is the appropriate time to get to know each other in a more relaxed atmosphere.

DURING YOUR VISITS AT THE CORPORATE CENTER, FOSTER YOUR NETWORK

Time was flying, and I had completely forgotten that I belonged to an international group of companies. I was just interested in my job and could not care less about our corporate center in Switzerland. I neglected to meet my network during each home leave and even declined opportunities to work there. All I wanted was to succeed as CEO with my company out there and to see our employees exploring their real potential.

In retrospect, this attitude was wrong; networking with the corporate center is vital for an expatriate's career. Somehow our success in difficult markets made its recognition at the corporate center without our conscious effort to sell our achievement. But I should have been more proactive and exploited offered options.

My commitment to the expatriate's career disallowed me to decline the next offer for Greece although I disliked leaving Asia. Anyhow, I negotiated my move to Greece under the condition to return to Asia upon completion of my CEO assignment in Greece.

THE MISTAKES DURING THE DEPARTURE IN INDONESIA WERE NOT REPEATED

This time, we packed our household stuff well ahead of our departure, and I accompanied Margrit and Goldy to Switzerland, where we rented a temporary residence. I returned to Malaysia and stayed for two weeks at the hotel, while the family was safely parked in Switzerland. It allowed me to complete my assignment in overdrive and with a sense of achievement to move on to the new assignment in Greece.

Greece, 1993 to 1996

1. Political and economic environment
The Greek government desperately wanted to make its mark in the European Union (EU); unemployment was high, and the economic development was one of the slowest in the EU.

2. Our group
We expanded our services to financial services with acquisitions of banks and asset-management companies, which made us lose the well-guarded AAA rating of the past.

BACK IN EUROPE, AT LEAST THAT'S WHAT I WAS TOLD

I flew from Malaysia directly to Thessaloniki, the head office of a newly acquired group of companies in Greece. From the "vibrant economic environment of Asia," I arrived in "dead Thessaloniki," a shock for which I did not properly prepare myself. All I knew about Greece was the due diligent report selling us the companies as market leaders.

Upon arrival, I asked the taxi driver to take me from the airport to the best hotel in town, which was Macedonia Plaza. By Asian standards, this hotel should have been pulled down many years back. For those readers who know the newly renovated Macedonia Plaza, I wish to be precise that I arrived shortly before its renovation. All was in a dark-brown color. I was tired from my trip, and I sank into the bed, whose sheet was covered with cigarette burns. The jet lag did not allow me to find instant sleep, and I wanted to pull the TV closer toward me, but the table caved in. I called the operator, and even after numerous calls, nobody showed up. That night made me feel like taking the next plane back to Asia.

But hold on—this was my next posting, and as an expatriate I had to make it here again.

The next day, I went to the office, and here again, I thought, "Where am I on this globe?" A life-threatening elevator took me up to our offices. There was hardly any light in the corridor. Whatever I looked at was overused and in total contrast to my nine years in Asia. People also looked at me as if I came from the moon, and my Asian positive can-do attitude didn't quite find its echo. At 4:00 PM sharp, our employees left the office for their luncheon with their families (not dinner), followed by their "holy siesta" until 8:00 PM. And close to midnight, we ate dinner with a lot of oil, bread, and more-often-cold meat until the early morning hours.

AND THE CULTURE SHOCK AGAIN KNOCKED ME TO THE FLOOR

This culture shock was by far greater than the culture shock I experienced in Indonesia or Malaysia. Hence, I wanted to deprive Margrit of this experience and told her to stay in Switzerland until I had settled down either in Thessaloniki or Athens.

The hate-love relationship between Thessaloniki and Athens was visible everywhere in both cities and within our companies. The people of Thessaloniki are more people-oriented, whereas Athenians are more business-minded. Finally, I decided on Athens due to its international focus, and we moved the head office from Thessaloniki to Athens. What a shock to our people in Thessaloniki who did not expect to lose against Athens.

My first impression of Athens was that this place must have just come out of a war. Its numerous unfinished houses had exposed corrugated irons, indicating either an extension, a stop of the construction, or a destruction of the building. Anyhow, this was now my new home, and I was well advised to immediately adjust my Asian view to the Greek environment.

NEVER ARGUE WITH INTUITION

Whatever I looked at in our companies was wrong and in sharp contrast to the due diligence report. A gut feeling and intuition told me to immediately fly to Switzerland, our corporate center, and propose an immediate withdrawal from the deal. After the first meeting, a good friend of mine quietly pulled me to his office and reminded me that I should be more careful in my approach. At first, I did not quite understand what he meant, but his further explanation was kind of an eye opener to me. My proposition was indeed offending those executives who agreed on the investment in Greece. I was just not capable anymore of successfully dealing with organizational politics and could not care less to also expose wrong decisions.

On the other hand, I truly liked being part of our group, and, hold on, there was also something like a career on the line. Hence, we worked out a compromise with the immediate sale of two companies and a commitment to rescue the operation with the highest option for profitability. It was kind of a saving-face deal but fell well short of my professional ambition.
For the first time in my career, I compromised on my standards, and I still hate myself for doing that—to argue with intuition.

WHAT GREAT BODY LANGUAGE GREEKS HAVE

You have to not understand Greek in order to understand Greeks. Their body language is indeed unique. The way they move their heads, roll their eyes, move their fingers, and lift up their shoulders is telling you everything. They are convinced of themselves and as a nation with an ancient history are very proud of their heritage. Generally speaking, Greeks like to smoke, drink, eat, and sing. As a result of such a lifestyle, they often look considerably older than their age. On the other hand, it is a nation that knows how to enjoy the moment.

A SMOOTH START AT A NEW ASSIGNMENT HELPS TO OVERCOME CULTURE SHOCK QUICKLY

After some months, we finally found the appropriate house on Ekali's hillside, some ten kilometers north of the city. It is worth the while not to compromise on the location for your house, because your family will spend most of their time at home, and expatriates work long hours. It is essential to have a harmonious family life at home, which makes the difference, in particular while living abroad. And indeed, Margrit felt very much at home in Ekali and in Greece. Margrit appreciated the long walks with our dog, the land turtles that came to our house (she marked them each year), and the splendid view from our house.

We experienced extreme climatic conditions with temperature as hot as 43° C, severe flooding, bushfire next to our house, and even snow of thirty centimeters.

The fiercest experience was the bushfire, and a street of four meters made it possible for our house to escape the flames. We learned from our experience in Indonesia and were this time well prepared for this emergency call in the middle of the night. Valuable things, passports, and flight tickets were all nicely packed in one suitcase together with some clothing. All we had to do was pick up the suitcase, rush to our car, and drive off to a safer destination.

SHALL WE CONTINUE WITH OUR EXPATRIATE CAREER?

The years in Greece stood as a crossroads in our expatriate career. Questions had to be answered, such as should we head back to Asia, stay with the group, settle down in Switzerland, start our own business, which place will we declare as our "final destination for retirement," etc.

Finally, we decided to stay with our group, to continue with the expatriate career, and we made the deliberate decision to make Switzerland our destination for retirement. While in Greece, we benefited from the vicinity to Switzerland, and we bought property in a prime location near Lucerne. My advice is to buy property only in prime locations, because you never know whether you will have to sell it again.

It is just natural, no matter how dirty your roots might be, to go back to your roots upon retirement. Some make such decisions at a rather late stage of their lives, and we did so at the age of forty-three. The roof of our new house was just completed when I was asked to move from Greece to India.

We packed again, but this time, we moved it to our not-yet-fully-completed house in Switzerland. Margrit made herself comfortable at "our final destination" (how much I hate these three words), and I took the next plane to Delhi.

India, 1996 to 1998

1. Economic and political environment
During this period, India started opening up to the world's economy. A number of industries were privatized, and a number of state monopolies were abolished.

2. Our group
We struggled to realize synergies between the existing organization and new acquisitions. Our group failed to merge the different corporate cultures into one common culture, and British as well as American executives started their fights for supremacy.

IT TURNED OUT DIFFERENTLY THAN WE PLANNED

I arrived in Delhi just to witness within the first month BJP's victory over the established Congress Party. This was an unexpected political change and caused the liberalization plans of the defeated Congress Party to stall. Indeed, there was no reason for me to stay in a hardship country with its high taxation and high cost of living for expatriates. Hence, we stopped the work permit process, and I stayed in the hotel, commuting between Switzerland and India.

Margrit caught up with her family in Switzerland, and we only met each other during my breaks in Switzerland. Long absences from home unfortunately also form an integral part of an expatriate's commitment.

The pollution in Delhi was life-threatening, causing us to often stay outdoors for just an hour a day. We sometimes did not even see the sun for days, and a complete inversion covered the city. Many of my expatriate colleagues with small children had to leave Delhi on a monthly basis to go to an environment with cleaner air. Today, all taxis and buses are banned from using diesel, and Delhi has returned to a green city.

My culture shock in India was due to the degree of indifference toward the immediate environment outside the doorstep of an Indian house. Within its own walls, a perfect world rules, whereas, generally speaking, Indians care less about environmental protection outside their homes. It is also difficult to understand obsolete acts, such as the rent act in Mumbai. For the benefit of readers who have never been in Mumbai, let me briefly explain what the rent act is all about. According to this act, a landlord is not allowed to increase the rent under which circumstances he does not find any more reasons to renovate the house. Hence, he will just wait until such a point in time that the house collapses, which makes Mumbai a city of old and ugly houses. The tenants will beautify their apartments but just to the doorstep.

I admired in India how people could cope with the magnitude of poverty and yet peacefully live together. Religious beliefs supported by the belief in Karma seemed to be the key for such success.

In front of our office in Mumbai was a traffic light, and whenever a truck with a water tank approached this traffic light, it turned red. Do not ask me how this was possible, but it was an obvious fact. The drivers had little choice but to wait until it turned green again. During this two-minute stop, children patiently collected the water drop by drop from the leaking tap at the rear of the truck's water tank. Excess water, which could not find its immediate consumption, was carefully collected in a larger pot.

While awaiting the liberalization of the insurance industry, we focused on the development of our asset-management company, and I found time to share a good time with Indians. Generally speaking, those professionals I worked with were extremely well educated and found it difficult to accept that foreigners could also be smart.

A TALENT POOL OF PEOPLE WITH THE HIGHEST ASPIRATIONS

What impressed me most was the great number of highly qualified professionals with great knowledge also outside their professions. It was just a pleasure to be inundated by their wisdom and knowledge.

I also interviewed a number of highly qualified professionals, and one of the applicants gave me the opportunity to attend his class. They studied under extreme conditions, and it was no wonder that they outperformed any of their competitors within an air-conditioned environment.

LISTEN TO THIS GREAT INDIAN WISDOM

On the way to a party some twenty kilometers outside Delhi, I had a great experience with a taxi driver. He honked every two hundred meters, and after a few "near misses," I suspected that there might be something wrong with his eyes. I wanted to be polite and gave him my invitation to read with the excuse that I did not quite understand the nature of the party. "Sir," he replied, "let me read it at the roadside," and he stopped his ambassador car. He took out from his shirt's pocket very big glasses, which looked more like goggles. He patiently read the card and explained each detail on the invitation. Upon completion of "his lesson," he put the goggles back in his pocket. Afraid of the continuation of our journey without the driver's glasses on his nose, I dared to ask him whether he would not prefer to wear the goggles, sorry, the spectacles. He turned his face toward me and replied, "Oh no, sir, they might break in case of an accident."

MY KARMA IS THAT INDIA IS NOT MEANT TO BE FOR ME

The expected liberalization was finally postponed to the year 2001, and I was offered the CEO position in the Philippines with a mutual commitment of returning to India upon the liberalization of the market.

The Philippines, 1998 to 2002

1. Economic and political situation

Under the political "leadership" of President Joseph Estrada (Erap), the economic development was severely stalled. Unlike in other Asian countries, the economic development in the Philippines ever since has been controlled by large family conglomerates that at the same time also control the political agenda.

2. Our merged group

With too many merged entities, our group finally lost its distinctive corporate culture. We reached troubled waters and lost within one year more than 80 percent of our market capitalization.

COMPLETE ABSENCE OF CULTURAL UNDERSTANDING AT THE TOP OF OUR MERGED GROUP

Our group's management decided to annex Australia to our Asia region. If one cultural mistake would not already be enough, it was also wrongly decided that Australia would lead our established Asian network as the regional management. To round up the cultural mistakes, Asia was asked to report to London instead of to the corporate center in Switzerland.

A number of very unfortunate cultural mistakes were committed by the group's executives who had no cultural understanding of Asia; neither did they have a commitment to Asia nor a successful track record of working with foreign cultures.

Generally speaking, Asians deeply mistrust Australians mainly due to Australia's anti-Asia immigration policy and Australia's insular thinking. Strategic growth markets like India and China, where one-third of the world's population are living, request the appropriate level of authority, which is only at the group's corporate center in Switzerland (from the Chinese/Indian point of view).

The authorities and future shareholders in such markets expected to deal only with the highest-ranking group executives at the corporate center and not with executives from a country they deeply mistrust. I make that point not to insult my dear Australian friends, but it is my intention to highlight the importance of cultural fits, which is often neglected in multinational companies. The same subtle cultural differences can be found among many cultures, and we are well advised to respect them.

We speak here of cultural barriers that cannot be overcome by professionalism. By Asian standards, Australia's market size is not worth talking about (a number of Asian cities have a higher population than Australia as a country). It will take years to overcome this cultural barrier, and a number of incidences including the Bali bombing in 2003 and the bombing of the Australian Embassy in Jakarta in 2004 serve as reminders of this serious cultural gap between Asia and Australia.

CULTURE SHOCK, WHERE ARE YOU THIS TIME?

The Philippines has been as of today the only country that spared me of culture shock, despite its complex economic and political environment. Our Asian know-how intuitively made us understand local dos and don'ts, and we immediately felt at home.

Unfortunately, the Philippines (as a country) doesn't have much to offer to ambitious professionals, and a great number of professionals join the ever-growing overseas Filipino community of 12 million. Their adaptability to other cultures and their English language skills make them the ideal workforce abroad. Whether as medical doctors, nurses, engineers, seamen, musicians, actors, domestic help, teachers, or IT professionals, all of them will outperform expectations if you treat them with respect.

I share the frustration of this great number of professionals deprived of their well-deserved income opportunities under past, current, and most likely future political leadership. This vicious cycle can only be broken by a strong political leadership, which has yet to emerge. I sincerely hope this will be sooner rather than later.

As in any industry in the Philippines, our insurance industry made every attempt to protect domestic players from international competition. I was often approached for cartel-like agreements, but we were not afraid of competition and outperformed the whole industry in a shrinking market. Within four years, we improved the ranking of our general insurance company from the number 114 position to the 10th. Such achievement is only possible in markets with sleeping competitors.

A UNIQUE CULTURAL MIX NOWHERE FOUND IN ASIA

Unique in Asia is the Filipino way of enjoying the moment. The Spanish influence with its macho image as well as the American touch of lifestyle found their ways into the original Filipino culture affiliated to the Malay culture. This unique mixture makes the Philippines a pleasant place to be in Asia.

Discipline is not the most popular topic, and with some pain, I introduced in our offices some degree of discipline. You will meet traffic signs in front of traffic lights that read, "Please stop—when red." The emphasis is on "please" rather than "red."

The salary is paid twice a month with most of the money immediately spent or distributed within their extended families. The Filipinos are still committed to supporting not just their immediate but also their extended families. Taking into consideration the high poverty rate (40 percent are living below the poverty line) and high unemployment rate, the obligation of income earners indeed stands out from the rest. Hence, lower income groups do not have much of a choice but to request girls and boys to sell their bodies. They do not consider this as prostitution but rather as an act for pure survival.

Hence, saving money seems foreign to most Filipinos, even for those who might have some money left after distribution. Despite that fact, they outperformed themselves with the newest model of hand phones, and Filipinos are absolutely world class in text- messaging. I even came across traffic signs in Manila that read, "Please do not text while crossing the street."

THE GREATEST SMILE I HAVE EVER MET

What I liked best in the Philippines was the degree of innovation in earning money and the sound of Filipinos' laughing, unknown in other Asian cultures. Certainly most Asian cultures' smiles embed and reflect unique warmness. But the Filipino's smile is not a silent smile. It is a demonstration of joy—the whole body is laughing, the eyes are wet, and tears are rolling down the cheeks.

Also the degree of innovation in earning money stood out from the rest and did not stop at the steps of our offices. A number of our employees were very committed to their jobs during office hours and to the same degree to the income after office hours. Some of them performed after office hours as singers; others were involved in trading, artwork, teaching, or call centers; and the more beautiful or handsome ones enjoyed a night with foreign friends.

On this topic, a jeepney driver much impressed me. He converted his jeepney during the day three times, addressing very different target groups. For those unfamiliar with jeepney cars, such cars can be best described as an oversized jeep used for the transportation of all kinds of goods/people. All of them are beautifully decorated by the owner's distinctive artwork.

One particular owner of a jeepney used his car in the early morning as a taxi; during lunchtime as a mobile kitchen serving rice, chicken (each day the same lunch), and Coca-Cola (the brand in the Philippines); and after office hours, he proudly used his car as a "happy hour beer bar." I never checked him out in the evening, most likely depriving me of a new dimension of innovation.

STRICT CATHOLICS AND PROUD OF THEIR NATION—THE FILIPINO WAY

"I am sorry" seems to be the most popular three words in the Philippines. It might be related to the Catholic religion, to which more than 90 percent of the Filipinos belong to. It struck me that these words were used for negligent slips of tongues as well as for the most serious offenses. It seems to be the "Amen" behind an unpleasant discussion similar to that after a confession in the church. It can drive inexperienced expatriates crazy, and after these words, you are well advised to accept the facts in whichever form they may be shaped in front of you.

Speeches and events will be preceded by a pledge to the flag of the Philippines, accompanied by the national anthem and followed by a prayer. Everybody can sing the national anthem, and all of them deeply believe in God, but this does not mean there is an absolute commitment to the country (in particular, if the income tax is involved) or to the church (in particular, if one has to lie).

GREAT ACTORS ON AND OFF THE STAGE

What we also enjoyed was listening to Filipino bands, whose performances were identical to the original, even taking into consideration the finest details such as accents. It would not be wrong to say that most Filipinos have a strong desire to express themselves.

During all of our company outings and festivities, we were never short of talent, and the artistic skill of Filipinos stands out from the rest. Filipinos, generally speaking, are great actors, not ashamed of letting their tears overflow their cheeks unlike in other Asian cultures I know.

IF YOU DO NOT LIKE YOUR RESIDENCE, DO MOVE

After one year at Dasmarinas Village, where most expatriates lived, we moved to Alabang, some twenty kilometers south of Manila. In particular, Margrit disliked Dasmarinas Village with its very old houses and leaking roofs, and we prematurely terminated the contract.

We replaced the home entertainment with frequent invitations to Peninsula, Mandarin, Gold Ranch, Shangri-La, and our golf club, Southwoods. Thanks to Werner Berger, the owner of Saentis (a delicatessen shop with branches all over Manila), we comfortably survived with the best of cheeses and wines from all over the world.

A GREAT NUMBER OF EXPATRIATES BUT NOT MUCH OF AN EXPATRIATE COMMUNITY LIFE

In comparison to other Asian countries, the expatriate community is large, the majority of which enjoys retirement in the Philippines. The low cost of living, in comparison to Europe, attracts many foreign citizens to retire in the Philippines. Certainly, contributing factors are the favorable weather conditions, the warm hospitality, and the beauty of the Philippines' women recognized at global beauty contests.

Expatriate life in the Philippines is very different from other Asian countries. It is kind of a loose relationship with fellow nationals with an open invitation to Filipinos. A great number of clubs exists in the Philippines with strict entrance codes for new members.

I was a member of the prestigious Matchstick Club under Hans Brumann's leadership, the famous jeweler in Manila. At the Peninsula Lobby, you could see them meeting each Thursday for lunch since Peninsula's foundation (1972).

I HAD LEARNED NOTHING IN GREECE, AND I AGAIN ARGUED WITH INTUITION

You might remember that I left India for the Philippines with a mutual commitment to return to India. My gut feeling intuitively reminded me of a past experience in India. But I trusted our key executives in London, who confirmed our group's commitment to India in a public speech in Delhi. I was also given the confirmation that our group's board at the corporate center firmly stood behind the approved investment for India.

Against my gut feeling, I argued that my gut feeling was just wrong and our employees and shareholders in India were eagerly waiting for my return to India.

HERE WE GO AGAIN; GOODBYE, PHILIPPINES

It was an emotional goodbye because we left many good friends behind, and it is just hard to say goodbye to Filipinos, too. Margrit left for Switzerland because she knew that the last few weeks of an expiring assignment and the first few months of any new assignment request for an around-the-clock commitment was best managed without family commitments. Hence, I left a few weeks later for India but this time for Mumbai instead of Delhi.

EXPATRIATES ARE OFTEN TOO LATE TO CONVEY A FINAL GOODBYE TO FRIENDS WHO PASS AWAY

Rather unfortunately, within weeks upon Margrit's arrival in Switzerland, her sister passed away. Such sad events haunt many expatriates' lives, and their stays abroad seldom allow them to be in time if family members or best friends are fading. Hence, they always arrive too late, and remorse haunts them for being too late. Anyhow, Margrit was this time at the right spot, whereas I again could not attend to the matter in the way my relationship to her sister called for.

India And Our Premature Departure To Switzerland, 2002

1. Political and economic environment

BJP was still in power, but the insurance market was finally liberalized and experienced the entry of most of the leading foreign insurance companies. Contrary to other Asian countries, the weak global economy had little impact on India's economy, mainly due to its large domestic market.

2. Our group

The balance sheet of our group was on a rather shaky foundation, leading to the early departure of our chairman and CEO, who had a strong commitment to strategic growth markets (India and China). US executives assumed management control with a strategic direction committed to markets they were familiar with (USA).

INDIA, HERE I AM AGAIN

Here I was again but this time in Mumbai. I was familiar with India as well as with my executive colleagues, whom I recruited back in '96-'98. We immediately started to establish the designed platform for planned composite operation (life, non-life insurance), and our existing asset-management companies continued to outperform the market.

But within a couple of months, we had to take note of our group's changed commitment for investments in strategic growth markets. It took all my energy to keep our people in India motivated toward our plans, and despite the strong rumor, we continued our work in a committed manner.

TOO MANY COWARDS IN THIS CORPORATE WORLD

After a local board meeting in Mumbai, my Australian colleague on the board of directors pulled me aside and conveyed London's decision to divest from India. It was not a shock to us, but we would have expected to hear this decision from those key executives who publicly confirmed our group's commitment to India just some months ago in India.

I recruited very capable key executives, uprooted their careers, and motivated them to work for a great group. I offered a continuation of my value creation in our group to our key executives in London, and my emails were not even answered!

As of this moment, I finally believed in my Karma, that I am not made for India.

ABSENCE OF CULTURAL UNDERSTANDING LEADS TO COSTLY MISTAKES

My poor Australian fellow desperately wanted to inform our JV partners of London's decision, and he flew to Delhi against my advice, that such drastic corrections in strategies have to be communicated to Indians in the Indian way. I am truly saddened that something like this could happen in our group because we would have had the cultural understanding to professionally manage the difficult situation.

EXPATRIATES' CAREERS ARE EXPOSED TO UNEXPECTED CHANGES

Expatriates' assignments, being of a temporary nature, are certainly more exposed to global changes than assignments embedded in a more stable corporate environment in the country of origin. Many of my colleagues were affected by erratic changes in strategies or changing priorities within their own families (mostly related to health issues or to children's education).

Lucky us, it was the first time after nineteen years abroad that it felt as though somebody pulled the carpet out from under my feet. Without having a commitment to children, we packed the suitcases, neither worrying about future loss of income nor future residence.

Here again, married expatriates without children and a house in the country of origin are the preferred choice for employers, because of the considerably lower costs for repatriation (e.g., saving on relocation costs, education for children, home leaves, taxes, and smaller local residences, etc.).

THIS TIME, NO FAREWELL PARTY, NO SENSE OF ACHIEVEMENT, NO FLOWERS

Our regional office in Australia gave me only three days to clear my desk and completely ignored my requests for a decent departure from India and my employees. Praveen and Anita accompanied me to the airport in Mumbai, and on the way, we shared some experiences of my foreign assignments. Anita said, "You really should put this down in a book," which was the trigger for this book. They labeled my final departure from India with a special note, which I treasure in the complete absence of any corporate gesture.

On a positive note, my departure to Switzerland allowed us to check out whether we would be able to adapt again to our inherent Swiss culture, dear to us upon our departure from Switzerland in 1984. We could now critically judge from a new horizon, shaped by the colors of our global assignments, whether we could make it in our country of origin.

BE AWARE OF THE REVERSE CULTURE SHOCK UPON YOUR ARRIVAL IN YOUR COUNTRY OF ORIGIN

Expatriates returning to their countries of origin also experience culture shock—called reverse culture shock.

This shock hits many expatriates much harder than culture shocks experienced in their foreign assignments. I was not exempted from this experience, whereas Margrit managed more successfully the return to our inherent culture.

Some of our expatriate friends even divorced upon the return to their country of origin, which was mainly caused by the reverse culture shock making them arguing around the clock. Where as those expatriates who are aware of this potential conflict upon their arrival in the country of origin find over time the appropriate solution on the way forward. A lot of patience and talking is advisable before venturing to a point of no return.

Most expatriates look forward to returning to their roots. But as they become once again part of their roots, they quickly realize that the experience abroad completely changed their perceptions of their home countries. Important is to first take note of this fact and understand that the expatriate has changed and not the home country. Hence, do not try to change your home country, which might be quite a task. Instead, define the gap between you and the prevailing culture in your home country. Manage these differences with patience until you arrive at an objective judgment before you define the way forward.

Switzerland, 2003

Here we were again, at the age of fifty-three, in Switzerland, the country we left at the age of thirty-four for our foreign assignments. What had changed in our home country since our departure in 1984?

1. Political and economic environment
I perceive Switzerland as a beautiful museum, and generally speaking, Swiss are not quite made for changes. They have a commitment to understatements, to an average performance, and always strive for consensus.

The political scene did not change much, whereas the global economy had its impact on Switzerland's economy with many industries completely revamped.

2. Our group
What a change—the AAA-rated icon of a Swiss multinational insurance group with its decentralized management structure in 1984 found its opposite replacement in 2003. I found a global financial service provider with a top-down management style and a group's balance sheet a far cry from what it was back in 1984.

BACK AT THE CORPORATE CENTER AFTER NINETEEN YEARS

Our head office in Switzerland greeted me in an unexpected manner. We hardly knew each other, and I wondered whether I entered the right building. It seemed that nobody was aware of my achievements, and I could greet neither our CEO/chairman nor my direct superior.

After twenty-four years with our group and six successful CEO assignments abroad, I first had to put together my CV and sell my managerial and professional expertise to unknown decision-makers at the corporate center. I could not have chosen a more inappropriate time for my return, because our group just kicked off a retrenchment program for more than 4,500 positions.

And the first group of people to look at is always the group of expatriates because their replacement with local management resources will immediately impact the expense ratio. Although, I doubt that this is a contribution to the sustainability of the bottom line.

At this point in time, I cannot put more emphasis on the importance of maintaining the network during an expatriate's assignment. At the corporate center, hardly anybody knows you, and without a network, you are considerably lost upon your return. I created my new assignment at the corporate center with my limited network and found a colleague who had to succeed on a specific management task for which my professional and managerial skills were tailored.

BACK AT OUR RESIDENCE

Here we were in our dear country of origin, although four years earlier than planned. The weather greeted us from its coldest side with minus zero temperatures and snow. At this stage, I wished to be a bear preparing for a long sleep and waking up in more familiar climatic conditions in spring.

People also had that serious look on their faces, and any exchange of words seemed to be inappropriate.

The weather and people I perceived as most difficult to manage upon my arrival. They paralyzed my positive can-do attitude, whereas Margrit was less affected.

In order to put the reverse culture shock in its right perspective, let us share some of our experiences to better understand this phenomenon.

I passed through customs' green lane (no declaration) with two bottles of cognac. Although I would have had ample space in my suitcase, I simply forgot to smuggle them well hidden in one of my bags. I was just too excited to be back home and looked forward to being in my house again together with Margrit.

The customs officer instantly spotted the bottles, and this was at 6:25 AM. He greeted me in a rather impolite manner, certainly not the most appropriate welcome after a long-haul flight. I was glad that Asia taught me how to remain friendly in such a situation.

The customs officer reminded me that I would only be allowed to import one of those bottles, and I found it the appropriate solution to offer him one bottle (free of charge of course). The body language immediately made me understand that my generosity was ill designed for a Swiss customs officer. He reminded me that he couldn't be bribed, which actually was not my intention. After a cumbersome calculation, he finally arrived at my charge of SF 16.20, an amount of money equal to four coffees. I wanted to quickly settle the fine in US dollars, a deal which he refused. He reminded me that he was not a bank, and I could not avoid reminding him that this airport seemed to me to be an international airport.

Instead, he requested that I get Swiss francs at the bank's counter, which I found closed for the next half-hour. But I noticed that the counter outside immigration was already open, and I asked the customs officer to let me pass through immigration in order to exchange my dollars to Swiss francs. He refused to accommodate my request, and I killed time with some espressos and also enjoyed a relaxing shower at the Alegra Lounge.

After one hour, I returned to customs and found no customs officers on duty. I finally found them behind shelves enjoying their coffee, too. Instead of welcoming me with a smile, he asked me about my whereabouts within the last hour. Here again, I kept my temper, as any Asian would do, mainly because the customs officer still was in possession of my passport. Finally, I could give him SF 20 and told him to keep the change, a proposal he again refused. Instead, he had to search among his colleagues for the appropriate change. Finally, he found the appropriate change, and I was enriched with the experience of "the unique hospitality" of my home country.

On my way home, I analyzed the customs officer's behavior as well as mine and concluded that anything in Switzerland is permitted that is not explicitly forbidden in writing. Generally speaking, people in Switzerland are rather on the stubborn side of life with a structured mindset deeply anchored in routine, disallowing them to deviate from procedures and rules.

On the other hand, how could I expect such a customs officer to appreciate my gift or to realize a capital gain from foreign exchange. That was just beyond that poor fellow's thinking, and his accent revealed his place of origin, the State of Wallis (Oberwallis to be precise), which is a valley surrounded by high mountains. This environment shaped his personality, and I had better take it into consideration the next time I pass immigration.

This experience made me aware of the fact that I had changed and certainly not the customs officer. Not even the international airport in Zurich would make him change his inherent cultural mindset.

BUT HOLD ON, THERE IS MORE TO COME

After many years abroad, some cleaning around our house had to be done, and I also cut some branches off our trees. The debris made a perfect fire, which I lit after sunset with a sense of achievement. Would you believe it? Within minutes, I received the company of a gentleman whose strong beam of his torch reminded me of a landing of an MD-11. He introduced himself as the fire brigade commander of the municipality and requested that I immediately distinguish the fire. He further explained that such debris had to be packed in plastic bags and could not be burned in the open. He even was able to quote the paragraph referring to my offense.

Here again, everything is permitted in Switzerland that is not explicitly forbidden in writing.

But I was the one who did not know such rules, and I am well advised to immediately attend a crash course on our municipality's rules, which is of course different from adjacent municipalities.

KEEP ON HOLDING YOUR BREATH; IT FOUND ITS CONTINUATION

In our region, we have some marders (a cute fox-like animal). One of my friendly neighbors gave me the hint to disperse some Carbolineum, the odor of which those animals dislike. Hence, I went to the pharmacy, purchased eight liters of Carbolineum, and dispersed it on my own property. Guess what happened. The next day, I saw on my property a member of a specialized troop called Oil-Detectors. He was dressed like a fisherman with high green boots, which were fixed on straps hanging from his shoulders. I quickly checked the calendar to see whether Carnival had already started. With the confirmation that there were still some days to go until Carnival, I dared to greet the gentleman.

He explained the reason for his unexpected appearance and reminded me of my serious offense of dispersing oil. I corrected him that it was Carbolineum, which made his face even whiter than his already-pale appearance. I also asked him how he became aware of my attempt to keep undesired animals off my property, and he told me that he had to act on behalf of one of our not-that-friendly neighbors.

Any Swiss seems to be a policeman, and I seriously considered canceling my burglary insurance. My neighbors seemed to closely survey my property day and night and would certainly alarm the police of any intruder.

Here again, my good old country did not change. I dared to do something which would have not even have caught the attention of hundreds of Asians.

I'd rather stop here, although some more stories could be added to this subject. The issue for expatriates is that they return to their home countries with the wrong expectations. They assume that they still know the cultures of their home countries, but they do not.

Their host countries changed their horizons, and my advice is to be patient. Do not aggressively test the limits of your fellow countrymen in your home country right upon your return to your country of origin.

I SIMPLY COULD NOT FIGURE OUT HOW THEY WORK AT THE CORPORATE CENTER

I enjoyed my assignment while traveling around the world, and lucky me, I was hardly in the office. I noted that I was a completely different person while on my journeys abroad from what I was at my office at the corporate center. At the corporate center, it felt like being in prison, and I felt so great while abroad acquiring partner companies for our group.

Although I was given fifteen months to complete my external partner company network, I made it in twelve months. The limited time I spent at the corporate center I used to establish my new network and succeeded in getting an offer for an assignment as CEO in Indonesia. Without thinking twice, I accepted the assignment, and I went back to Indonesia, where I had started my international career some twenty years ago.

Margrit also established her new network in Switzerland, and she wanted to stay in Switzerland. Well, we respected each other's different preferences, and I moved to Indonesia, whereas Margrit stayed in Switzerland.

Indonesia, 2004 to 2007

1. Political and economic environment
The socioeconomic environment completely changed with an outspoken young generation strongly requesting fundamental changes with high expectations to the newly elected President SBY.

2. Our group
Our group divested from a number of strategic growth markets with a commitment to the core businesses. It remained a great group to work for, although the journey to the AAA rating would be challenging.

INDONESIA, HERE I AM AGAIN

I met a great number of old friends again. The countryside did not change much, whereas Jakarta became more crowded with many new landmarks. I perceived the corruption level to be higher as well as the cost of living. To my surprise, fundamentally nothing had changed, and I immediately felt at home again.

OUR GROUP'S INDIFFERENT VIEW AND MY PERSONAL VIEW

In sharp contradiction to our group's strategic direction to be a global leader on international program business, our group divested from fifteen countries with an indifferent view on Indonesia. I convinced our group of Indonesia's strategic importance, and we proved with our financial result the viability for our group's investment.

MISSION ACCOMPLISHED

Our group's renewed commitment to strategic growth markets provided me with a great sense of achievement, and it felt as if my career just started again. At a crossroads, I did not know how long I would stay in Indonesia, but what I did know was that we would deliver superior results in the years ahead.

In looking back on the years abroad, I do not regret one single year. Born to be free remains my focus, and the expatriate life provides ample opportunities to fully experience this unique feeling.

It is either BINGO or DISASTER—the choice depends entirely on the expatriate's decision and the company's commitment to explore the inherent potential of expatriates.

Let me introduce the ten golden rules for a successful expatriate assignment.

Ten Commandments for Becoming a Best-selling Expatriate Part II

---

1. Do not neglect to foster networks at the corporate center or in your country of origin.

Expatriate assignments are of a temporary nature, and upon the successful achievement of an assigned management task, you have to move on to another expatriate assignment or return to your country of origin (the legal entity that sent you abroad). It will not take very long and your name will not be known anymore in your home country, and newly appointed key executives will not even be familiar with your achievements.

Hence, it is vital to constantly network in your home country or within your group of companies. Your chosen network should know your main achievements and try to socialize with the entire family. The longer you stay abroad, the more important such a network will become, and personal relationships can work wonders.

2. Provide your family with roots within your inherent or chosen culture.

It is certainly a great advantage if your partner has the same cultural background. But in an international community, more often than not, partners do not share the same cultural background.

In both cases, it is important that your family establishes roots either in your inherent culture or in the culture of your family's choice. Such roots provide a sense of belonging to your children and your family's life. The language spoken in your chosen family culture should be declared as your family language. Families who do not commit early to such a strategy will end up with serious difficulties, either already during their stays abroad or upon their return to the country of origin. We often asked expatriates' children the question, "Where do you feel at home?" and we received within the same family very different destinations (and cultures), indicating some troubles ahead for a harmonious family life.

3.   What can I best do with that pile of money?

It goes without saying that a foreign service employment will provide multiple earning opportunities to your salary in your home country. This is either the golden opportunity to save money or to spend it in your host countries. A number of expatriate friends bought luxury boats, and others made a comfortable savings. The choice is yours, and you decide the strategy without regrets.

Back home, you are certainly excited to share your experience abroad, and it is understandable that you want to also share your excitement with your family. Be aware that you address an audience who does not have servants, swimming pools, spacious housing, and company drivers who will pick them up for work.

We stopped showing photos and shared a good wine instead of talking too much about our standard of living abroad.

4. The higher standard of living abroad.

You are certainly mature enough to understand that your higher standard of living will be of a temporary nature, but your children might not be fully aware of that. They will attend international schools, not have much to help with at home, and readily accept the way money is spent in the "expatriate children community." It is important to keep your children on a realistic platform and remind them of the temporary nature of your expatriate assignment.

5. Managing "both" culture shocks.
You will differently experience culture shock in each new country. Either it will take you and your family just a few weeks to overcome such culture shock or it will stay with you as a nightmare during the full period of your assignment.

The greatest of all culture shocks you will experience is upon your return to your country of origin. The so-called "reverse culture shock" upon your return to your country of origin will hit you far harder than you ever could imagine. You have tremendously widened your horizons abroad and you acquired an international mindset that has little in common with your previous domestic mindset.
Just be aware that you are the one who changed and not your fellow countrymen.

Do not underestimate culture shocks and systematically cure them. Each member of your family will experience it very differently, because all of you are exposed to different issues although all of you live in the same host country.

6. Strictly no involvement in political activities in your host country.
As an expatriate, you have to respect your host country's political and social environment. Any active involvement on the political scene will put at risk your family, you, and your business development. Hence, stay away from political activities and never express publicly your political view.

7. Select your residence in your host country according to your family's preference.
While staying abroad, it is vital to have a harmonious family life, and

all family members have to feel at home in your temporary residence. The "non-working partner" and your children should have the veto right to any location/house proposed by your company. Do stay firm and move to another location if the family does not immediately feel at home.

8. Keep your "non-working partner" involved in your businesses.
More often than not, expatriate postings end because the partner does not feel at home in the host country or is not occupied or properly involved in the daily activities of her/his spouse. Hence, it is important that you make your partner part of your busy schedule and that she/he is known to your business partners. If she/he establishes her/his own network, try also to be part of it.

9. Get the focus right on the education of children.
Very often, the education of children will dictate the length of your foreign assignment. Hence, carefully synchronize your career as an expatriate with your children's education. Select a school system that will be compatible to your family's culture of choice or the most likely destination upon expiration of your foreign assignment. Expatriates with children are expensive for employers, and expatriates without children are certainly the preferred choice.

10. Keep in touch with your expatriate colleagues.
Upon return to your home country, you will most likely realize that you will not have much in common with your friends anymore, except the memory you share with them prior to your departure. Your horizon abroad tremendously widened, and your focus dramatically changed. The old friends were not exposed to a global environment, and they are still deeply anchored in their own domestic world. Try to retain the relationships gained in your host countries and foster this network, because they understand your world, share valuable memories, and stand on the very same platform.

Proposal for a Foreign Assignment Contract Part III

——➤•◀——

1. Introduction

An expatriate is by definition a professional who is committed to the know-how transfer within a multinational organization. He/she attends to a specific management task for which the <u>local expertise in the host country is not (yet) available.</u>

From the expatriate's point of view, the incentive for the foreign assignment should be to benefit from an attractive remuneration package and to fast-track his managerial, professional, and multicultural development.

The employment status during the foreign assignment shall remain as employee of the legal entity from which the expatriate left for the foreign assignment. Important is that the expatriate remains anchored in the pension plan and social security of the home country, allowing an easier integration upon the return to the country of origin (called home country).

Prior to the departure, it must be made clear to the expatriate that the company wishes to   continue employment upon the successful completion of the foreign assignment. But such employment cannot be guaranteed upon departure. Employees who insist on guarantees are not made for an expatriate career, which requires an entrepreneurial spirit and the passion to explore uncharted waters.

Generally speaking, the expatriate's remuneration is split into the salary received in the host country and the salary received in the home country. The expatriate's total salary package takes into consideration the cost of living differentials between the home country and the host country. Also considered is the fact that the partner of the expatriate might not be able to pursue a professional career, and families with children need particular attention for the education of the children.

Hence, it is obvious that there is <u>no uniform approach to expatriates' remuneration</u> packages. Rather, each package is tailored to the specific circumstances in the home and host countries, as well as to the expatriate's specific situation.

Generally speaking, the following elements form part of an expatriate's remuneration package:
- the underlying contract with the home country's legal entity delegating the expatriate to the foreign assignment and
- the local contract with the legal entity in the host country.

Both contracts can be merged into one agreement as outlined in my following proposal.

2. Remuneration, benefits, and allowances in both countries (home and host)

2.1. Remuneration received in the home country and the host country
- 2.1.1. Remuneration paid in the home country

The remuneration paid in the home country consists of the fixed salary paid in the home country and foreign service allowance taking into consideration the specific circumstances of the respective host country.

Such remuneration is often a tax-free income to the expatriate because most countries just tax the income received in the country of residence (which is the host country). Carefully check the tax issue because an increasing number of host countries will request the declaration of the worldwide income.

The intention of the remuneration paid in the home country is meant to be the saving component within the total remuneration package.

- 2.1.2. Remuneration paid in the host country
The local remuneration paid in the host country consists of the local fixed salary and its performance-related incentives (linked to the achievements in the host country). The local fixed salary and performance incentives are always subject to local income tax in the host country.

The local salary and incentives should be in line with the local payroll and meant to cover the expatriate's expenses incurred in the host country.

Apart from above-mentioned split in remuneration, a number of multinational companies also define a notional salary, which is the salary used as the assessable salary for pension-plan-related benefits and its contributions. Not only will this salary count for pension benefits in the home country but might also serve upon return to the home country as a yardstick for the salary level.

3. Benefits received in the host country
Such benefits are country specific and are, generally speaking, costs related to moving, traveling, housing, transportation (cars), temporary residence, and home leave. My proposal includes possible benefits to a senior executive such as a car and club membership.

4. Allowances paid in the host country
These allowances may be related to the children's education, to the

study of the local languages, and to club memberships.

Every expatriate's package is tailored to specific circumstances and the company's intended strategy, and therefore, a wide variance exists. I came across solutions where the host country paid the total remuneration (mainly practiced by local companies with a mature presence in local markets) or where the larger part of the total remuneration was paid in the home country (mainly practiced for start-up operations and project-related assignments).
The company will have to find the best capital-efficient solution, taking into account the balance sheet of both legal entities (in the home country as well as in the host country).

Generally speaking, the total cost to the company for either approach will be more or less the same, whereas from the expatriate's point of view, tax-related advantages speak well for a split in remuneration.

I am pleased to introduce a possible letter of assignment for a foreign assignment contract, which may serve as your starting point in the design of a tailor-made contract.

5. Proposal of a LETTER OF ASSIGNMENT (insert specific reference at mark ".")

Dear "...."
We are pleased to confirm in this Letter of Assignment the offer made to you between "legal entity of the home country" (hereafter referred to as L-Home) and "legal entity of the host country", in "country" (hereafter referred to as 'the Company').

You will be appointed to the position of "designation" based at offices in "address of company in the host country". Your local employment will be established with the Company.

The assignment is expected to last for approximately "number of years". This letter of assignment shall be supplementary to your current employment agreement with "L-Home" and will replace the terms and conditions of your current assignment letter.

The main conditions are as follows:

Starting date: The start date is to be effective "date" or as and when requested by your manager.

Permits: The Company will initiate the process in "country" for the appropriate permits to reside and work in "country".

Reporting line: To the "designation", a position currently held by "name of superior".

Home country: "country".
Host country: "country".

Salaries per annum: As of the commencement of your assignment in "country", your fixed remuneration is composed as follows:

1.1. A gross salary of "currency and amount" per annum, payable in your host country in twelve monthly installments; and
1.2. A gross salary of "currency and amount" per annum, payable in your home country in twelve monthly installments.

Notional salary: As of "date", your notional salary will be "currency of home country and amount" per annum. This amount will count for pension benefits in your home country.

Foreign service
allowance: As of "date", you will be paid a foreign service allowance of "currency of home

country and amount" per annum to be paid
in your home country.

Compensation
review:
Your compensation arrangements will be
reviewed in line with the policies applying
in your home country and in your host
country.
Your notional salary and home salary will be
reviewed in line with the practices in your
home country, and your local salary in the
host country will be reviewed in line with
local practices of the Company. The first
review will take place "date".

Incentive
compensation:
For the performance "year" (full incentive
award to be paid by the
Company in your host country), your award
will be determined in
accordance with the objectives agreement
agreed upon by your manager. The target
incentive will be "percentage" of your
notional salary.

Pension plan:
You will remain in the pension plan in your
home country. The notional salary will form
the basis for benefits and contributions.

Social security:
You will remain in the social security plan
of your home country. You have agreed to
be exempted from similar plans in your host
country.

Medical insurance:
You should remain enrolled in your medical
plan arrangements in your home country
and be ensured of global coverage. The
Company will reimburse you the cost for
you and your family.

Vacation and home leave:	While working in your host country, you will be eligible for "days" annual vacation. You are entitled to one home leave trip to your home country, based on "class of fare" for you and your family per calendar year, paid by the Company.
	When possible, home leave should be combined with business trips to your home country. Home leave not taken within the available period will automatically lapse, unless otherwise agreed in writing. Home leave cannot be taken as a cash payment in lieu of an actual trip.
Relocation assistance:	The costs of travel and the shipping of household goods including insurance, up to a maximum forty-foot container, from "countries" will be paid by the Company.
	The Company will reimburse you the actual expenses incurred in connection with your relocation to your host country. All expenses will be reimbursed in the host country.
Housing:	The Company will provide you with a mutually agreed-upon company-leased accommodation. The cost of all utilities and phone rental will be your responsibility. The Company will bear the costs of taxes charged in relation to the provision of housing.
Schooling for children:	The Company will pay the yearly school fee for your children at an international school

in the host country.

Company car: You will be entitled to the use of a company car plus a driver in your host country. All maintenance, taxes, insurance, and running costs will be borne by the Company.

Club membership: The Company will provide one corporate club membership in your host country and reimburse you for regular monthly dues as well as for business use of the club.

Taxes: The filing of income tax returns and the payment of income taxes according to the tax law in your host country on your salary and salary-related income benefits are your responsibility. The Company shall deduct taxes at the source in your host country. The tax on your income in your home country may be due on a monthly basis or upon declaration of your annual income.
All tax advice and filing related to your assignment in your host country will be performed by the Company's tax advisors, the costs of which will be borne by the Company. If you choose to utilize a tax counselor other than those services provided by the Company, the cost of such services would be borne by you.

Local conditions: While working in your host country, you will be expected to comply with the requirements of local laws and local conditions of employment.

Repatriation: The Company will pay for the repatriation costs according to the "L-Home" corporate guidelines. This will include travel, shipment and storage of household goods, temporary living, and repatriation allowance.

Termination of international assignment:	Upon successful completion of your assignment, the group is in principle prepared to offer you a new assignment, commensurate with your education and occupational experience and abilities. The search for such assignment will begin approximately five months before the expiration of your assignment.

Either you or the group may terminate the international assignment agreement by either party giving the other party three months' notice in writing. Such notice will take effect at the end of three months when notice is received. During this period, the full assignment package will continue to be paid.

Your underlying employment contract with "L-Home" requires either party to give "months" notice in writing to terminate employment. This may be given concurrently with the notice period of the international assignment agreement. During the balance of the notice period, the notional salary will form the basis of the compensation to be paid.

If you resign for reasons other than accepting a position with another employer or your employment is terminated prior to the contemplated end of the assignment, the Company will, within "months" of the termination, bear the expenses of your repatriation back to your home country, including the shipment of personal effects.

Applicable law   The laws of your home country will continue to apply and be the place of jurisdiction.

We wish you a challenging and successful assignment in your host country and look forward to supporting you in your stay abroad.

Yours sincerely,
"name/signature"

I have read the above "Letter of Assignment" and accept the assignment under these conditions.   Date:
                                                                                        Signature